CODES AND CIPHERS

JEAN COOKE

Wayland

SIGNS & SYMBOLS ➤

Body Language
Codes and Ciphers
Communicating by Signs
Writing and Numbers

First published in 1990 by
Wayland (Publishers) Ltd.
61 Western Road, Hove
East Sussex BN3 1JD, England

© Copyright 1990 Wayland (Publishers) Ltd.

Series Originator: Theodore Rowland-Entwistle
Series Editor: Mike Hirst
Series Designer: Michael Morey

Cover   A morse operator sending out a radio
message to shipping.

British Library Cataloguing in Publication Data
Cooke, Jean, 1929–
   Codes and ciphers.
   1. Codes & ciphers
   I. Title II. Series
   001.5'4 '36

   ISBN 1–85210–858–4

Typeset by Rachel Gibbs, Wayland
Printed and bound in Italy by
L.E.G.O. S.p.A., Vicenza.

CONTENTS

All the words that appear in **bold** are explained in the glossary on page 30.

KEEPING IT SECRET

Have you ever wanted to send a secret message to one of your friends? Do you ever write each other letters that no one else can understand? The best way to send a secret message is to make up a code or cipher.

Codes are not used just to send secret messages. They can make road signs easier to understand. Even if you can not speak the languages on this sign, you can

still work out what it means.

A code is a word or sign that has a special, usually secret meaning. To enter a headquarters, a soldier may need to know a secret code word, such as 'open sesame' or 'grey wolf'.

Ciphers are a more complicated kind of code, and are a way of sending longer secret messages. In a cipher, each letter or sign of a message stands for some other letter or sign. For example, you could make a simple cipher by **substituting** each letter of a word with the next letter of the alphabet; so the message,

AMBUSH!

would be written,

BNCVTI!

When we think about codes and ciphers, we usually imagine that they are used by spies and secret agents. But in fact, almost everyone uses codes every day. Codes may not even be secret at all. They can be a way of **abbreviating** information, or of sending a message quickly. At sea, ships can send messages to one another using special flag codes. Radio messages are often sent in a series of dots and dashes called morse code. On the street,

If you have a bicycle, you might fasten it with a combination lock to stop it being stolen. The numbers on a combination lock are a secret code.

road signs are a kind of code that all drivers need to understand. If you have a combination lock for a bicycle, the numbers that open it are a type of code too.

Keep a look out for some other codes. You will find them in the supermarket, in the library and on maps. There is even one on the back of this book. Can you spot it?

Break the Code

Can you crack this coded message?

LDDS ADMDZSG SGD NZJ
SQDD ZS ETKK LNNM

Turn to page 31 for the decoded message.

IN THE SHOPS: BAR CODES

Can you see the code on the back cover of this book? It is a pattern of thick and thin lines and is called a bar code.

On books, the bar code stands for a special kind of number, the International Standard Book Number, or ISBN. Every new book

Next time you go to a supermarket, watch the person at the checkout. Do they use a computer which reads the bar codes?

has one of these numbers. By reading the bar code, a computer can tell the name of the book and the author who wrote it.

To read a bar code, a **laser beam** scans the dark bars and the light spaces in between. The laser then turns the pattern into tiny pulses of electric current, which a computer can read.

Bar codes appear on many objects besides books, and there are several bar-code systems. The

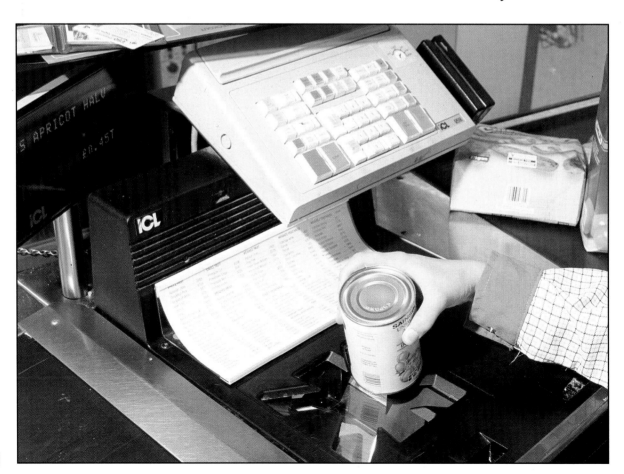

By using bar codes and computers, supermarket managers can tell if stocks of any food are running low.

most widely used one is called the Universal Product Code (UPC). You can often see it being used in supermarkets.

Nearly all goods sold in supermarkets today have bar codes on them, and shop computers use bar codes to give them a lot of information. Suppose you are buying a can of baked beans. When you come to the check-out desk, the shop assistant passes the can over a little window which has a laser reader inside. The bar code tells the computer that you have bought a certain size and brand of beans. The computer has the price of that can in its memory, and it prints the price on your receipt in the cash register. The computer also tells the shop's storeroom that another can has been sold. Then, when the stock of beans has almost run out, the storeroom computer automatically orders some more.

IN THE LIBRARY

When you go to the library to choose a book, look at the spines of the books. You will probably see some numbers on them, perhaps like this: 638.1. These numbers are part of a special code that librarians use to decide in what order the books should be placed on the shelves. It is called the Dewey Decimal System, and it was invented by an American librarian named Melvil Dewey in 1876.

If you are looking for a book on a particular subject, a chart like this one will tell you its number in the Dewey Decimal System.

Melvil Dewey divided all books into ten basic groups. He gave each of these groups numbers

When you know the number of a book, you can easily find it on the shelves.

between 000 and 999. For example, the numbers between 600 and 699 cover technology. Within the technology section, there are smaller groups of books; the numbers 630-639 cover books about agriculture or farming. The agriculture section is then split up even further.

How would the Dewey System work for the number 638.1? The number 638 covers insects that make substances that are useful to us, such as honey and silk. To break down the numbers even further, Dewey put a decimal point after his three-figure

numbers, and so made a whole range of smaller groups. The number 638.1 covers books about beekeeping. If you want to find a book on silkworms, you look under 638.2, and so on.

Story books, or fiction, come in the group of numbers 800-899 which covers literature. But most libraries store all their story books in **alphabetical order** under the surnames of authors. So if you wanted to find the book *The Lion, the Witch and the Wardrobe*, you would look for it under the letter 'L' for the name of the author, C. S. Lewis.

THE INTERNATIONAL FLAG CODE

Flags are a useful way of sending messages. They are particularly important for communicating at sea, and there is an international flag code which ships can use to send messages.

The international flag code is illustrated on the facing page. As you can see, it has square flags for each letter of the alphabet, and triangular **pennants** for the numbers 0–9.

When signalling, sailors **hoist** groups of between one and five flags. Many flags or groups of flags have special meanings. For example, a ship that is about to weigh anchor and leave port hoists the flag for 'P', commonly called the Blue Peter. RY means, 'My crew has mutinied.' NC means, 'I am in distress and need immediate help.' AD means, 'I must abandon ship.'

Nowadays, ships send most messages by radio, but flags are still a good way of sending messages over short distances. The international flag code is also very useful for ships in foreign waters, where the captain may want to signal to someone who does not speak the same language. The international flag code book explains the code in nine languages: English, French, German, Greek, Italian, Japanese, Norwegian, Russian and Spanish.

Flags flying from a cruise liner. The two flags on the right show that the ship is just arriving at port.

The International Flag Code

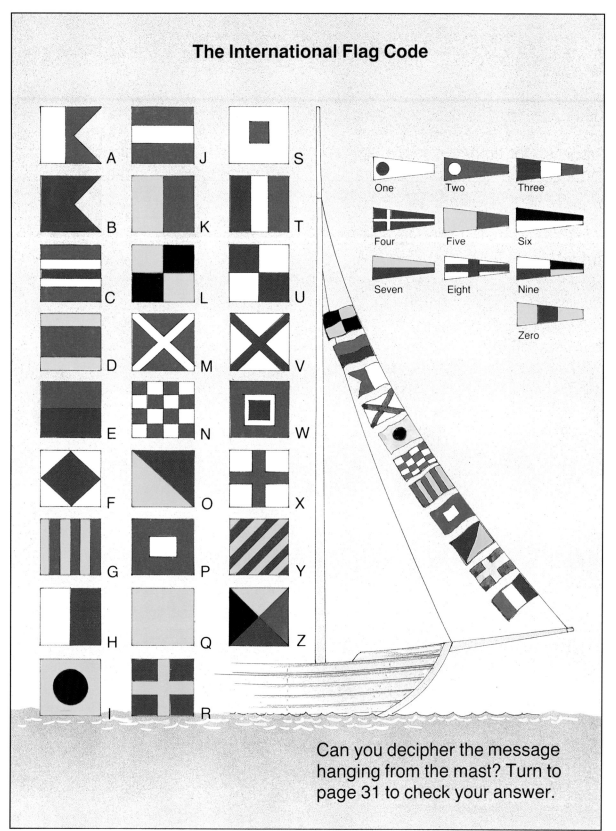

Can you decipher the message hanging from the mast? Turn to page 31 to check your answer.

SEMAPHORE SIGNALS

Semaphore is another way of using flags to send messages. Unlike the international flag code, you do not need many different flags to send semaphore signals. Semaphore uses just two flags, and different letters of the alphabet are made by a person holding the two flags in different positions. The semaphore alphabet is shown on the opposite page.

The first semaphore signals did not actually use flags at all, but were made by placing mechanical arms in different positions. This early semaphore system was invented in 1793 by Claude Chappe, a French engineer. He wanted to find a way of sending messages quickly from Paris to other European cities. He built a string of towers on high ground. On top of each tower was a mast with two mechanical arms. The position of these arms could be changed from the ground by a series of **winches**. During the day, someone with a telescope would keep a look-out, and when they saw a message on a tower in the distance, they would read it and then pass it on to the next tower down the line.

When the **electric telegraph** was invented, semaphore towers were no longer used, but other people were already adapting the invention for their own needs. Railway engineers used the idea of semaphore arms for railway signals. At sea, the modern semaphore code was developed using flags. Even today, this code is an important way of sending messages when ships have to keep radio silence.

This engraving, from the early nineteenth century, shows one of Claude Chappe's semaphore towers.

The Semaphore Alphabet

A	G	N	U
B	H	O	V
C	I	P	W
D	J	Q	X
E	K	R	Y
F	L	S	Z
	M	T	

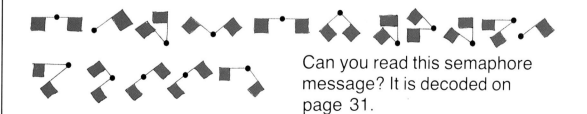

Can you read this semaphore message? It is decoded on page 31.

MORSE CODE

The morse code is a code of dots and dashes used in signalling. In this code, long and short buzzes are used to stand for letters of the alphabet .

The inventor of the morse code was not a professional scientist, but an American artist, Samuel Morse. He invented his code in 1838, to transmit messages through one of the earliest electric telegraphs.

Up until the 1920s, people used morse code for sending messages over telegraph wires. Then, after the invention of radio, the code was used by radio operators for long-distance signalling. Even today, the sound of morse can carry well through **radio interference**.

The most famous morse-code message is the special signal for 'Help!' - three dots, three dashes and three dots which make the letters S,O,S (Save Our Souls). The message has brought rescuers to the scenes of many disasters.

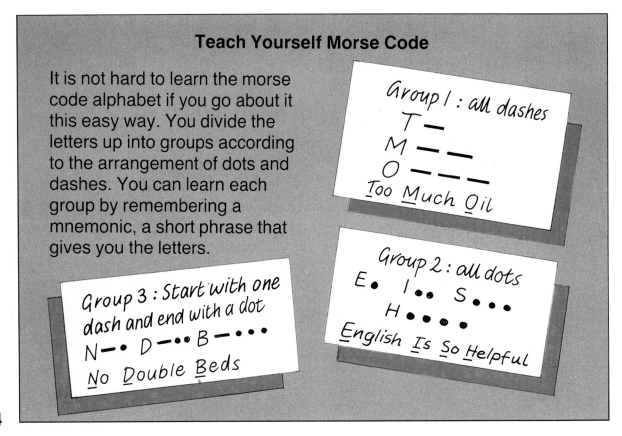

Teach Yourself Morse Code

It is not hard to learn the morse code alphabet if you go about it this easy way. You divide the letters up into groups according to the arrangement of dots and dashes. You can learn each group by remembering a mnemonic, a short phrase that gives you the letters.

Group 1 : all dashes
T —
M — —
O — — —
<u>T</u>oo <u>M</u>uch <u>O</u>il

Group 2 : all dots
E •   I • •   S • • •
H • • • •
<u>E</u>nglish <u>I</u>s <u>S</u>o <u>H</u>elpful

Group 3 : Start with one dash and end with a dot
N —• D —•• B —•••
<u>N</u>o <u>D</u>ouble <u>B</u>eds

Group 4 : Begin with two dashes and end with a dot

G — — •

Z — — • •

<u>G</u>ambia <u>Z</u>ambia

Group 5 : Start with one dot and end with a dash

A • —   W • — —

J • — — —

<u>A</u>nnoying <u>W</u>ireless <u>J</u>ams

Group 6 : Begin with two or three dots and end with a dash

U • • —   V • • • —

<u>U</u>ltra <u>V</u>iolet

Group 7 : Begin with one or more dashes and end with a dash

K — • —   Y — • — —

X — • • —   Q — — • —

<u>K</u>eep <u>Y</u>our <u>X</u>ylophone <u>Q</u>uiet

Group 8 : Begin with one or more dots and end with a dot

R • — •   L • — • •

P • — — •   F • • — •

<u>R</u>ich <u>L</u>ondoners <u>p</u>refer <u>F</u>ish

Group 9

C — • — •

<u>C</u>onclusion

What is the meaning of this morse code message?

Turn to page 31 for the decoded sentence.

CHEMICAL CODES

Have you ever seen the code H2O? It looks mysterious. But in fact it is a common symbol, used by scientists to describe an everyday substance. H2O is the chemical formula for water. Scientists use this formula because it is an easy way of writing a lot of information about water.

Everything on earth is made up of atoms, tiny particles of special chemicals called elements. There are 109 of these elements and they are joined together in different ways to make rocks, plants, animals and even the air we breathe. Ninety-two of these elements occur naturally, and scientists have made seventeen other ones in laboratories.

Each element has a name, but some of the names are very long

Have you ever seen a chart like this? It is called the periodic table, and lists the chemical symbol for each of the elements.

Many everyday substances can be written down as a chemical formula. This boy is sprinkling NaCl (salt) on his bag of chips.

and so each element has an **abbreviation** too. In the symbol for water, H stands for the chemical hydrogen, and O stands for oxygen. The numbers in a chemical formula tell us the amount of each element in a substance. In H_2O, the number 2 shows that there are two atoms, or tiny particles, of hydrogen for every one atom of oxygen.

Water is only one of the everyday substances which has a simple chemical formula. We can write the names of many of the foods that we eat in chemical codes too. Next time you sprinkle salt on a plate of chips, try to remember the chemical formula for salt. Chemists call salt sodium chloride, and its formula is NaCl. Na is the symbol for sodium (from the Latin word *natrium*) and Cl is the chemical symbol for chlorine. In salt, there is one sodium atom for every atom of chlorine.

MAPS AND THEIR CODES

Maps are full of codes, and before you can read a map, you first need to understand the meaning of all the special symbols. Some symbols are quite easy to work out; a cross, for instance, usually stands for a church. Other signs are not so obvious. You may have to look at the key printed at the side of the map to find out what they mean.

Most maps are drawn to scale, so that we can tell what distances are covered by the map. If the scale is 2 cm to 1 km, every 2 cm on the map will show one kilometre on the ground. The scale is often written as a **ratio**, such as 1:100,000. In this scale, 1 cm on the map equals 100,000 cm (or 1 km) on the ground.

Many maps also show the height of the land, using contour lines. Can you see these lines on the map opposite? They are spaced a regular distance apart, usually every 50 m, and they join together all the places that are the same height. From the shape of the contour lines, you can tell where there are mountains, hills and valleys. When the lines are spaced

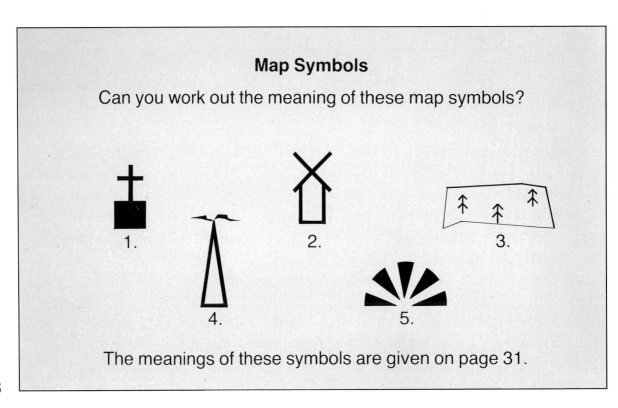

Map Symbols

Can you work out the meaning of these map symbols?

1.

2.

3.

4.

5.

The meanings of these symbols are given on page 31.

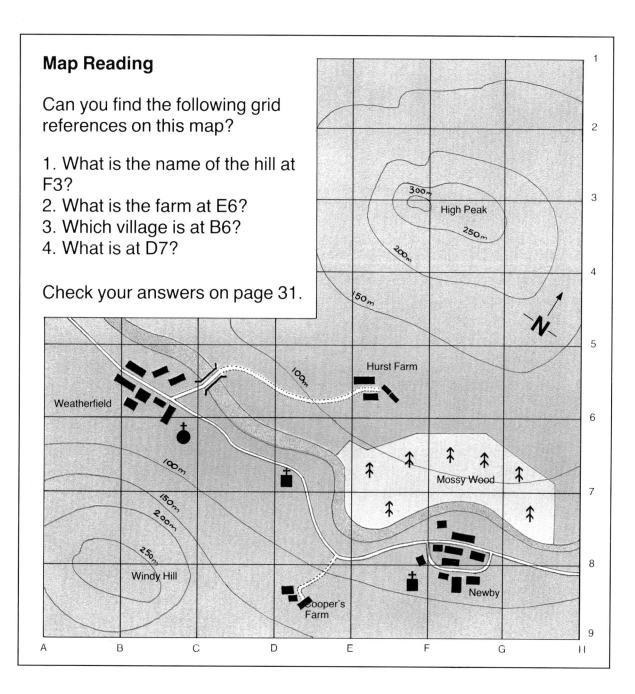

Map Reading

Can you find the following grid references on this map?

1. What is the name of the hill at F3?
2. What is the farm at E6?
3. Which village is at B6?
4. What is at D7?

Check your answers on page 31.

High Peak

300m

250m

200m

150m

Hurst Farm

100m

Weatherfield

100m

Mossy Wood

150m

200m

250m

Windy Hill

Newby

Cooper's
Farm

A   B   C   D   E   F   G   H

1 2 3 4 5 6 7 8 9

close together, it means that there is a very steep slope. However, when the contour lines are spaced wide apart, the land slopes only gently or is almost flat.

Every map has a grid of fine lines across it. These lines are marked with letters or numbers in the margin, and they help you to find places on the map easily. Look at the map above. Can you find grid reference point F8? First find grid line F and then follow it along until it meets grid line 8. What is the name of the village that you can see there?

19

MAKING A MAP

Large maps are drawn by teams of experts. The first stage is to survey, or plot the ground. The surveyors use long tapes and instruments to measure distances and angles, and work out the height of mountains and valleys. The height of land is always measured in metres above sea level. The work of the surveyors on the ground is helped by photographs taken from aeroplanes or **satellites**.

When all the information has been gathered, the map is drawn by special artists called **cartographers**. They decide what features they are going to show, and what codes they will use on the map and in the key. Many cartographers now use computers to help them draw maps.

There are many different kinds of map, which show different kinds of information. A political map shows the boundaries of countries and states, and the position of cities. A physical map shows the natural features of a piece of land, its mountains, rivers, woods and lakes. Some maps have special uses. A road map shows motorists how to find their way, and other maps contain information about population, climate or air routes. Geological maps are drawn in many different colours, to show which rocks lie underground.

Make Your Own Map

You will need: Coloured pencils

Paper

Make a sketch map of the area where you live. (A sketch map is a map that is not drawn to scale.) First, draw in the roads and streets. Next, mark the houses and other buildings. You can also include: woodland; parks; fields; churches and other religious buildings; schools; post offices; public houses; telephone boxes; railway lines and railway stations; rivers and lakes; bridges. Use different coloured pencils to show different things. For instance, parks could be marked in green and rivers in blue. Beneath your map, make a key to explain the symbols you have used.

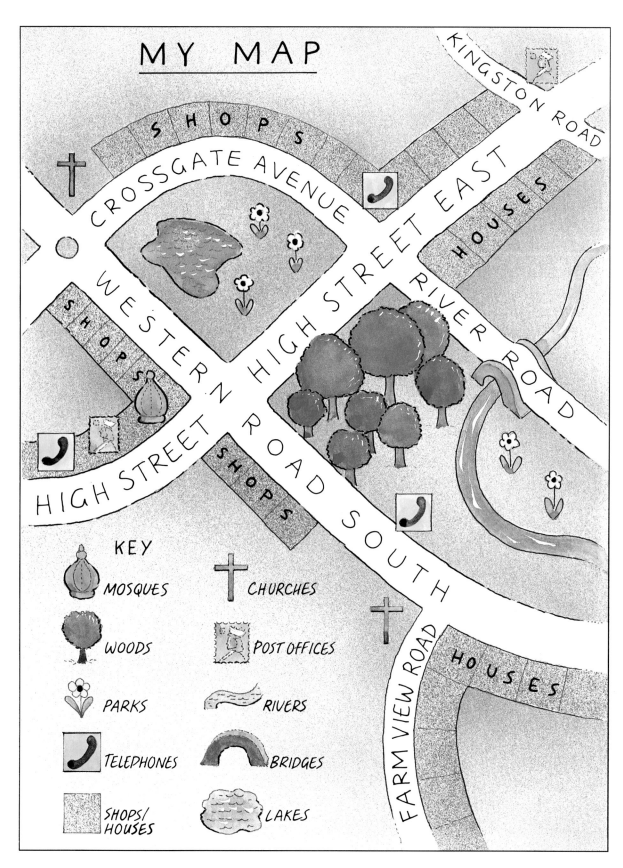

MY MAP

KINGSTON ROAD

SHOPS

CROSSGATE AVENUE

HIGH STREET EAST

HOUSES

RIVER ROAD

WESTERN

HIGH STREET

SHOPS

ROAD SOUTH

SHOPS

HIGH STREET

FARM VIEW ROAD

HOUSES

KEY

MOSQUES

CHURCHES

WOODS

POST OFFICES

PARKS

RIVERS

TELEPHONES

BRIDGES

SHOPS/
HOUSES

LAKES

ORIENTEERING

If you know how a map works and can understand the kinds of codes that map-makers use, you can try the sport of orienteering. The name of the sport comes from the word 'orientation', which means finding out where you are. In orienteering, the competitors have to find their way as quickly as possible over a difficult course, using maps and compasses.

To be good at orienteering, you have to be able to run well over rough ground. But even more important, you must be able to read a map properly.

When the competitors set off, they are given a map of the course, a compass and a sheet of paper with the map references for the control points. The competitors have to find their way from one

A competitor at an orienteering meeting rushes towards the next checkpoint.

control point to the next. As they go, they mark the route in red pen on their maps. At each control point there is an official who stamps the competitors' cards to show that they have been there.

The control points are positioned so that you can not see from one to another. To know which way to run, you must take compass bearings. First, look on the map to see where the next control point is,

Taking a compass reading.

and draw a straight line between it and where you are standing. Lay the map flat, and put the compass on it so that the needle points to the north. Then turn the map around until the north marked on the map is the same as the north on the compass. The line that you have drawn will be pointing in the direction in which you should run.

WEATHER MAPS

You probably see a weather map every day, either on television or in a newspaper. These maps are made by **meteorologists**, who study the weather. They gather information about weather conditions from weather balloons, ships, satellites and local weather stations all around the world. They then put all of this information down on a weather chart.

Most weather maps contain simple symbols, which show if the weather will be sunny, wet or cloudy. The temperature is usually marked in degrees celsius at a

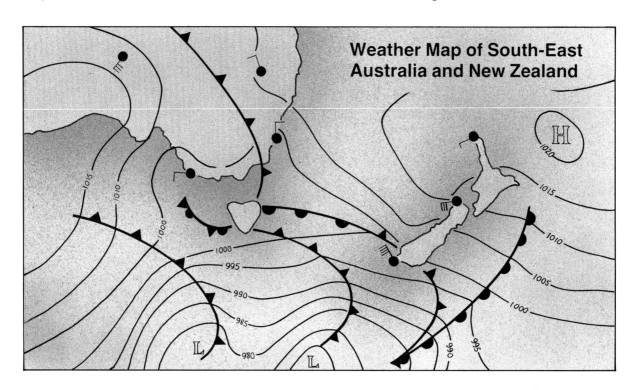

Weather Map of South-East Australia and New Zealand

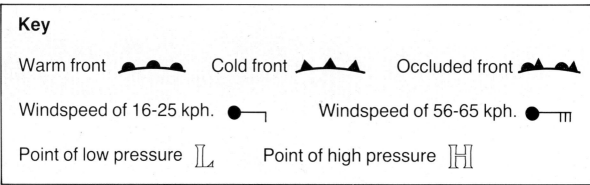

Key

Warm front ● ● ●   Cold front ▲ ▲ ▲   Occluded front ▲ ● ▲ ●

Windspeed of 16-25 kph. ●—   Windspeed of 56-65 kph. ●—ııı

Point of low pressure L   Point of high pressure H

Next time you see a weather forecast on television, see how many of the special symbols you can recognize.

number of points on the map. Some maps also contain signs which give the wind speed. The direction of the wind is marked by a stick pointing out of a circle. The strength of the wind is shown by the number of tails on the stick. It is particularly important that sailors know about wind speeds, in case any gales or strong winds blow up while they are at sea.

Another important piece of information on a weather map is the air pressure. Meteorologists measure the areas of high and low pressure, and from this they can predict what the weather will be like. On weather charts, pressure is shown in isobars, lines which connect all the points with the same air pressure. The highest and lowest points are also marked on the map, usually with a capital letter L or H.

At the places where high and low pressure meet, fronts are formed. If the air is warm, it is called a warm front, and is marked on the weather map by a thick line with semicircles pointing in the direction in which the front is travelling. If the air is cold, the cold front is marked by a thick line with triangles. Sometimes a cold front meets a warm front, and pushes the warm air upwards. The front is then called an occluded front, and is marked by a line with both semicircles and triangles. When a front passes over an area of land, it almost always brings a change in the weather.

SIMPLE CIPHERS

There are many ways of making up a cipher. One of the commonest is to find a code word in which there are no two letters the same, for example the word EXPLAIN. Write the code word, followed by all the remaining letters of the alphabet in order. Then write the alphabet above it correctly, like this:

```
A B C D E F G H I J K L M
E X P L A I N B C D F G H

N O P Q R S T U V W X Y Z
J K M O Q R S T U V W Y Z
```

If you want to write the message, 'Meet me at midnight' in cipher, find the letters in the upper row and substitute those in the lower row. The result will be:

HAAS   HA   ES   HCLJCNBS

To make the coded message even harder to crack, you could then break up the words in the wrong place, so that your message looks like this:

HA   ASH   AESHC   LJCNBS

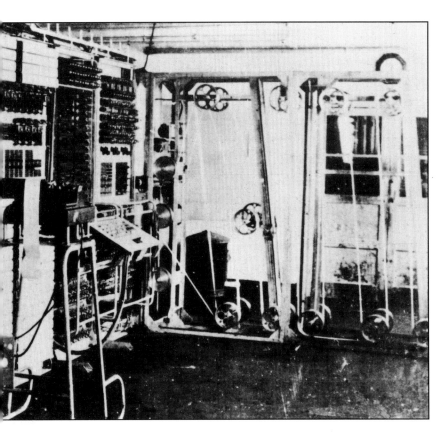

Colossus, one of the first computers in the world, was invented by Dr Tommy Flowers. Using his computer, Dr Flowers was able to decipher the top-secret codes sent by the German military during the Second World War.

A Grid Cipher

Here is another easy cipher. Make up a grid like this:

Then put the dots in place of the letters like this:

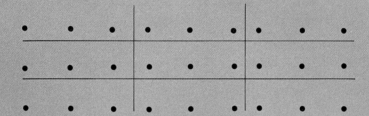

When you write your message, draw the appropriate part of the grid and just put a dot where the letter should be:

• ⌐| = A   ⌐•| = B

So the message, 'Meet me at midnight', becomes:

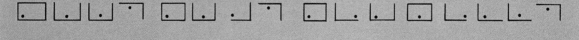

Can you decode this message?

Turn to page 31 to see if you are right.

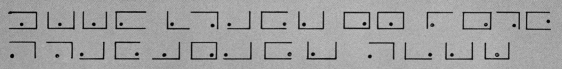

SPIES IN ACTION

Spies use codes and ciphers all the time. They are issued with code books, which contain the codes that they need to send secret messages. The code books are very valuable and must be kept out of enemy hands at all costs.

During the Second World War, British sailors captured several German code books from sunken submarines. Using these books, the intelligence service was able to read German radio messages sent to ships at sea. Many important messages were intercepted and the Allied forces were able to **predict** German naval movements.

Every intelligence service has a group of people who spend their time trying to crack codes, and most codes can be deciphered given enough time and a little luck. For example, the code breakers could look at a message to see which letters occurred most often. They might then assume that these letters stood for vowels. Or they may look for combinations of letters in a message. Three letters which appeared together frequently might stand for a common word such as 'the' or 'and'. Today, computers can do a lot of this **laborious** code-breaking work.

Some spies have been caught because their coded messages have been deciphered, but other secret agents have been more successful. One of the most famous of modern spies was Kim Philby. He became a senior British intelligence officer but was also in fact a **double agent** who passed information to the USSR. When he began to fear that he would be discovered, he fled to Moscow. It was not until several months later that the British managed to decipher a coded message proving that Philby was a double agent.

Even today people are fascinated by the spy Kim Philby, and there have been plays and films based upon his life story.

Above Morse machines are used every day to send out coded messages.

Right The badge of the United States' secret service, called the Central Intelligence Agency (CIA).

GLOSSARY

Abbreviating Shortening a word or phrase.

Abbreviation The shortened form of a word or phrase.

Alphabetical order Following the order of the letters in the alphabet.

Cartographer A person who makes maps.

Double agent A person who spies for one country while pretending to spy for another.

Electric telegraph A system of sending electric signals along a wire.

Hoist To lift something or raise it up.

Laborious Difficult and involving hard work.

Laser beam An intense, narrow beam of light.

Meteorologist A person who studies the weather.

Pennant A triangular-shaped flag.

Predict To say in advance what will happen.

Radio interference Hissing and crackling noises on the radio which are caused when radio signals are jumbled together.

Ratio The amount of one thing compared to another.

Satellite A spacecraft which moves around the Earth or other planet.

Substituting Replacing one thing with another.

Winch A device for lifting things.

PICTURE ACKNOWLEDGEMENTS

Allsport 22; Barnaby's Picture Library 10; BBC Enterprises 25; British Telecom cover, 26, 29 (above); Eye Ubiquitous 4; Sainsbury's Plc. 6, 7; Paul Seheult 5, 8, 9, 16, 17, 23; Topham Picture Library 28; Wayland Picture Library 12, 29 (below). All artwork is by Stephen Wheele.

BOOKS TO READ

Flags by Theodore Rowland-Entwistle (Wayland, 1987)
Loads of Codes and Secret Ciphers by Paul B. Janeczko (Grafton Books, 1986)

Message Detective by John Satchwell (Walker Books, 1985)
The Secret Service by Theodore Rowland-Entwistle (Wayland, 1987)

DID YOU BREAK THE CODES?

How many of the coded messages did you manage to crack?

Page 5:   *Meet beneath the oak tree at full moon.*

Page 11:   *Leaving port.*

Page 13:   *Return to the hills.*

Page 15:   *Telephone wires cut down the line.*

Page 18:   1. Church
               2. Windmill
               3. Coniferous forest
               4. Radio or television transmitter
               5. Viewpoint

Page 19:   1. High Peak
               2. Hurst Farm
               3. Weatherfield
               4. A church

Page 27:   *Keep guard on your starboard side.*

INDEX